For Finn and Zoë
—L. F. M.

National Geographic gratefully acknowledges the assistance of the National Aquarium.

This material is based upon work supported by the National Science Foundation under Grant No. DRL-1114251. Any opinions, findings, and conclusions or recommendations expressed in this material are those of the author(s) and do not necessarily reflect the views of the National Science Foundation.

As seen on the National Geographic Channel

Published by National Geographic Partners, LLC, Washington, DC 20036.

Design by YAY! Design

Trade paperback ISBN: 978-1-4263-1047-8
Reinforced library binding ISBN: 978-1-4263-1048-5

NGIC=National Geographic Image Collection; NGYS=National Geographic Your Shot

Cover, Charles Hood/Oceans Image/Photoshot; 1, Espen Rekdal/Blue Planet Archive; 4, Ocean/Corbis; 6, Jim Watt/Perspectives/ Getty Images; 8, David Shale/Nature Picture Library; 9 (UP), Michael Patrick O'Neill/NGYS/NGIC; 9 (LO), Scott Costa/NGYS/NGIC; 11, Stephen Frink/Science Faction/Getty Images; 12-13, Norbert Wu/Minden Pictures; 14, Jason Edwards/NGIC; 15, Solvin Zankl/ Blue Planet Archive; 16-17, Norbert Wu/Minden Pictures; 18 (UP), Dorling Kindersley RF/Getty Images; 18 (LO), Bill Curtsinger/ NGIC; 19, Norbert Wu/Minden Pictures; 20-21, Jeffrey de Guzman/NGYS/NGIC; 22, David Doubilet/NGIC; 23, Howard St. Quintin/ NGYS/NGIC; 24-25, Dordo Brnobic/NGYS/NGIC; 25, Gerald & Buff Corsi/Getty Images; 27, Emory Kristof/NGIC; 28, Susan Dabritz/ Blue Planet Archive; 29, Kerryn Parkinson/NORFANZ/Newscom; 30 (UP), Jason Edwards/NGIC; 30 (CTR), Emory Kristof/NGIC; 30 (LO), Scott Costa/NGYS/NGIC; 31 (UP LE), Jeffrey de Guzman/NGYS/NGIC; 31 (UP RT), Jon Milnes/Shutterstock; 31 (CTR), zebra0209/Shutterstock; 31 (LO), Colin Parker/NGYS/NGIC; 32 (UP LE), Jason Edwards/NGIC; 32 (UP RT), Michael Patrick O'Neill/ NGYS/NGIC; 32 (CTR LE), Stephen Frink/Digital Vision/Getty Images; 32 (CTR RT), Norbert Wu/Minden Pictures; 32 (LO LE), Emory Kristof/NGIC; 32 (LO RT), Jeffrey de Guzman/NGYS/NGIC; (header throughout), Petr Vaclacek/Shutterstock

Table of Contents

Strange But True. 4

Survival Skills 6

Hide and Seek 10

Big Eyes. 12

Making Light 14

Expert Food Finders 16

Deadly Dangers 20

Strange Senses 24

Super Subs! 26

Stump Your Parents. 30

Glossary 32

balloonfish

Many strange sea creatures live in the ocean.

Some are beautiful. Some are ugly. Some are cute, and some are scary.

Weird sea creatures are strange for a reason. The funny way they look and the strange things they do help them live in the ocean.

Survival Skills

Snorkeling in
shallow water

diagonal butterflyfish

Some sea animals live in the shallow ocean waters. Some live in the deep ocean.

The ocean can be a hard place to live. Deep areas are cold and dark. It can be hard to find food.

And the ocean can be dangerous. There are many predators. Any animal can quickly become dinner for another animal.

Water Word

PREDATOR: An animal that hunts and eats other animals

Sea creatures have special skills that help them find food. They also have strange body parts that can help them hide and stay safe from other animals.

How weird are these sea creatures? Let's find out!

eye

A Dumbo octopus finds food on the ocean floor with its large eyes.

A leafy sea dragon blends in with the seaweed around it.

A moray eel's sharp teeth catch prey.

Hide and Seek

Camouflage (KAM-uh-flazh) helps animals hide from their enemies. Looking strange helps them blend in to the plants or water around them.

Camouflage also helps animals catch dinner. Do you see the stonefish in the picture? Most fish don't because it looks like rock or coral. When they swim too close, the stonefish springs from the ocean floor. It grabs dinner in a flash.

Water Word
CAMOUFLAGE: An animal's natural color or form that blends in with what is around it

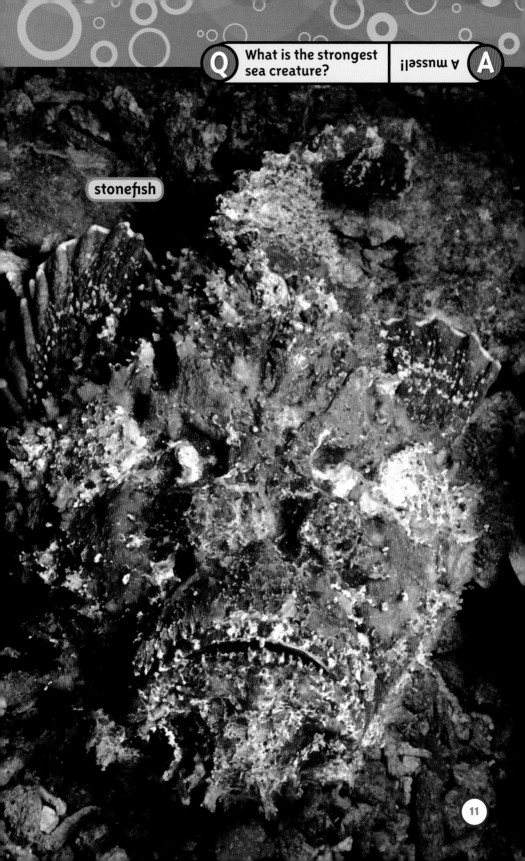

stonefish

Big Eyes

The deep ocean gets very little light. Many animals that live there have large eyes. Big eyes help creatures see in the darkness and find prey.

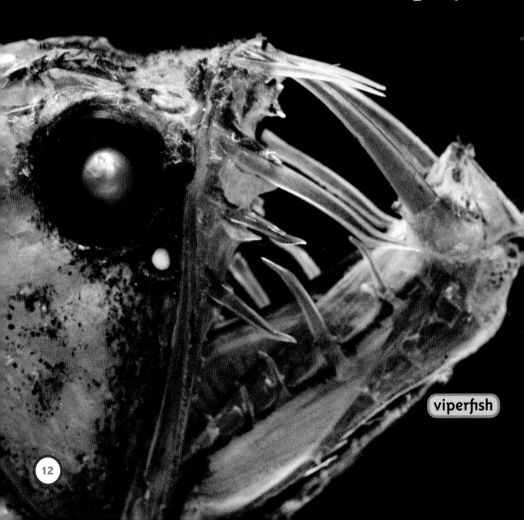

viperfish

hatchetfish

This viperfish used its big eyes to spot a hatchetfish. Dinnertime!

The hatchetfish uses its own large eyes to find tiny shrimp to eat in the dark sea.

Water Word

PREY: An animal that is eaten by another animal

Making Light

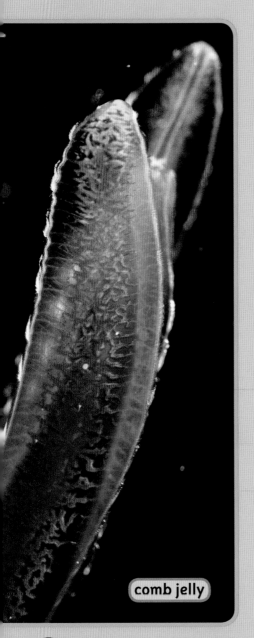

comb jelly

Many creatures in the deep, dark sea have a special trick—they make their own light! This is called bioluminescence (BYE-oh-loom-i-NESS-ants).

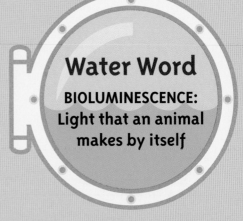

Water Word

BIOLUMINESCENCE: Light that an animal makes by itself

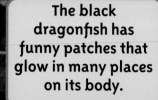

The black dragonfish has funny patches that glow in many places on its body.

Some sea creatures use their own light as a flashlight to find prey. Light can draw prey toward an animal, too. And light can surprise enemies, so an animal can make a quick escape.

patch that glows

Expert Food Finders

Some animals have wacky body parts that help them catch meals.

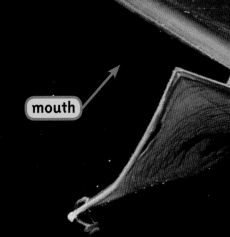

mouth

gulper eel

The gulper eel has a super-long tail. Prey comes closer for a better look. This eel's giant mouth opens wide. It can eat an animal bigger than it is. It can't be picky. In the deep sea, the eel must eat whatever it can find.

tail

The tiny cookie-cutter shark locks onto its prey with strange sucking lips. Its sharp teeth sink in. They leave a bite the shape of a circle.

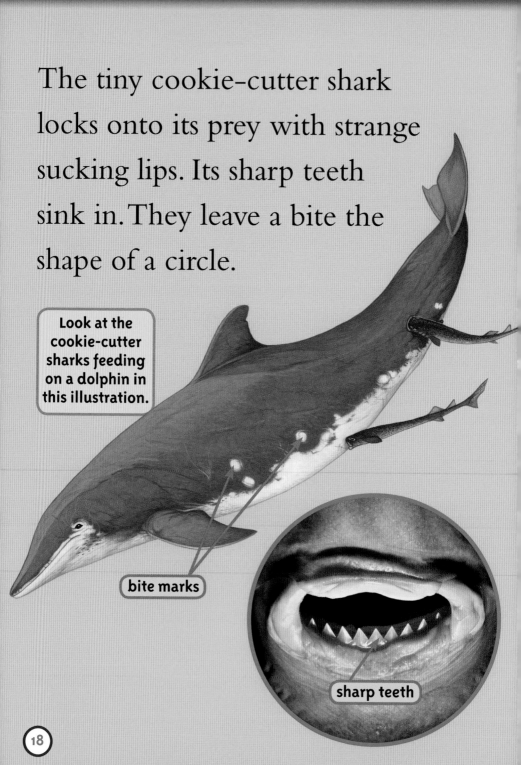

Look at the cookie-cutter sharks feeding on a dolphin in this illustration.

bite marks

sharp teeth

fishing lure

anglerfish

An anglerfish has its own fishing pole called a lure. The lure glows, and other fish want to know what it is. When they get close, the anglerfish eats them.

Deadly Dangers

Bumping into some sea creatures can be bad news.

The yellow sea anemone (ah-NEM-oh-nee) looks like a pretty flower. But it has stinging parts that have deadly venom. When a fish is stung, its muscles stop working. Then the anemone eats the fish.

yellow sea anemone

Water Word

VENOM: A liquid some animals make that can cause stinging, pain, or death

21

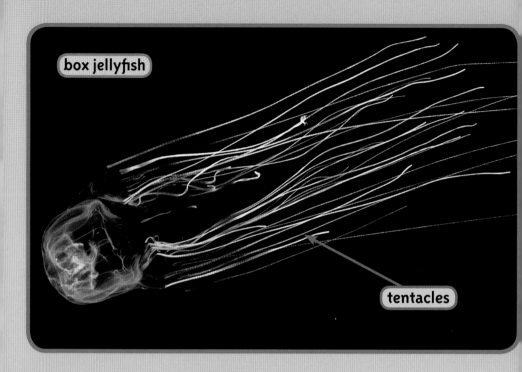

box jellyfish

tentacles

The box jellyfish is one of the most dangerous animals in the world. It has arms called tentacles (TEN-tah-kullz) that grow up to ten feet long. The tentacles deliver a painful, deadly sting.

This lionfish has crazy spiky fins. But you wouldn't want to touch them. The fins on its back are sharp and can sting you.

fins with venom

lionfish

Strange Senses

Some animals near the ocean floor don't even have eyes! They can't see their food. So they use other senses to find it.

A sea cucumber can feel tiny pieces of food stuck to its tube feet. It curls its feet in and licks them clean.

sea cucumber

hagfish

A hagfish has a super strong sense of smell and touch. It can smell food that's fallen from higher up in the ocean. It also uses feelers to find meals.

Super Subs!

How do we know about weird sea creatures in the deep ocean?

People can't dive deep to see these strange creatures. It's too cold and dark there. And the water pressure is strong enough to crush a person.

But humans can use machines called submersibles (sub-MER-sih-bullz) to explore the deep ocean.

Sometimes people control them from far away, like a remote-controlled car. And sometimes people ride inside.

14,764 feet

How Deep?

This submersible, named Alvin, can dive 14,764 feet deep. It would take more than 10 Empire State Buildings stacked up to reach that depth.

These odd tube worms live on the bottom of the ocean. They can grow to be eight feet tall.

Submersibles collect information. They have lights and special tools. They take pictures, and they gather plants, rocks, and animals.

Scientists used submersibles to find the weird creatures shown here. And there are probably thousands more that have not been found yet.

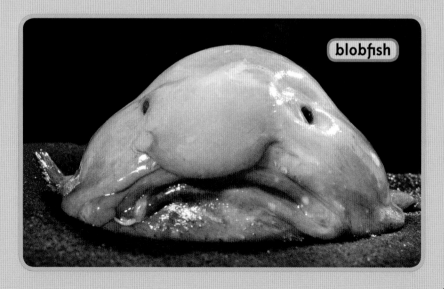

blobfish

Stump Your Parents

Can your parents answer these questions about sea creatures? You might know more than they do!

Answers are at the bottom of page 31.

1

Bioluminescence is _____.

A. a loud sound
B. the light an animal makes
C. a search for food
D. a fast swim

2

Machines that dive deep in the ocean are called _____.

A. speedboats
B. planes
C. submersibles
D. scuba suits

3

Which features are common in deep-sea animals?

A. big mouth
B. big teeth
C. big eyes
D. all of the above

Animals that have venom are _____.

A. not harmful
B. friendly
C. able to cause stinging, pain, or death
D. only found in shallow waters

Humans can't scuba dive deep into the ocean because _____.

A. it's too cold
B. it's too dark
C. the pressure is too great
D. all of the above

What is camouflage?

A. a way of eating
B. a way to blend in and hide
C. how animals see in the dark
D. none of the above

An animal that is eaten by another animal is called _____.

A. prey
B. an anemone
C. a tentacle
D. a creature

Answers: 1) B, 2) C, 3) D, 4) C, 5) D, 6) B, 7) A

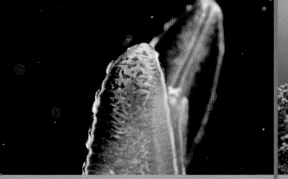

BIOLUMINESCENCE: Light that an animal makes by itself

CAMOUFLAGE: An animal's natural color or form that blends in with what is around it

PREDATOR: An animal that hunts and eats other animals

PREY: An animal that is eaten by another animal

SUBMERSIBLE: An underwater craft used to explore and gather information

VENOM: A liquid some animals make that can cause stinging, pain, or death